MONICA TEURLINGS

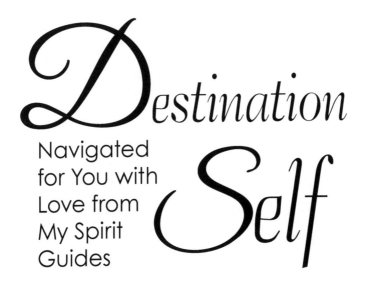

Destination

Navigated
for You with
Love from
My Spirit
Guides

Self

BALBOA.
PRESS

A DIVISION OF HAY HOUSE

Balboa Press books may be ordered through
booksellers or by contacting:

Balboa Press
A Division of Hay House
1663 Liberty Drive
Bloomington, IN 47403
www.balboapress.com
1 (877) 407-4847

Because of the dynamic nature of the Internet, any web addresses or
links contained in this book may have changed since publication and
may no longer be valid. The views expressed in this work are solely those
of the author and do not necessarily reflect the views of the publisher,
and the publisher hereby disclaims any responsibility for them.

The author of this book does not dispense medical advice or
prescribe the use of any technique as a form of treatment for
physical, emotional, or medical problems without the advice of a
physician, either directly or indirectly. The intent of the author is only
to offer information of a general nature to help you in your quest for
emotional and spiritual well-being. In the event you use any of the
information in this book for yourself, which is your constitutional right,
the author and the publisher assume no responsibility for your actions.

Any people depicted in stock imagery provided by Getty Images are
models, and such images are being used for illustrative purposes only.
Certain stock imagery © Getty Images.

Print information available on the last page.

ISBN: 978-1-9822-0073-2 (sc)
ISBN: 978-1-9822-0075-6 (hc)
ISBN: 978-1-9822-0074-9 (e)

Library of Congress Control Number: 2018903464

Balboa Press rev. date: 04/04/2018

Contents

Preface

I was around five or six when I had my first experience with a spirit guide.

Once I was tucked into bed for the night, my parents would argue—loudly. The anxiety this caused not only resulted in difficulty sleeping, of course, but also in some childhood trauma.

One evening as I lay in bed, a man appeared in my room, clear as day. He sat on the floor across from my bed and just stared at me from underneath his hat. He never approached me and never said anything, but somehow, I felt calm with him around and found that I could actually sleep whenever he made an appearance. Once my parents separated and we moved out of the house, I never really saw him again, though the memory remains strong even after all these years.

As time marched on and I became a teenager, I discovered I had a way of simply knowing things. Sometimes it was knowing what people would say before they said it, or who'd be on the other side of the door when the doorbell rang. I played this game with myself when the phone rang to see if I could predict who was calling. I was often right. I could foretell minor events before they happened or know when someone was being dishonest or less than genuine. I could also tell when someone was hurting emotionally. This was all normal for me. The running joke among my friends was that I was a little psychic.

I married at twenty-two, to a man nineteen years my senior. We had two gorgeous boys by the time I was twenty-five. For most of my twenties, I was a stay-at-home mom in suburbia. We divorced when I was twenty-eight, and now I was a single mom. It was the toughest time of my life. I had no husband and two kids to take care of by myself, with little money, no health insurance, no child support or alimony, no career, and few options.

The day we split, my ex-husband said to me (just as the U-Haul was about to pull away with most of our home furnishings in it) that I was nothing without him. That I would be in the gutter without him, and no one would want me. And what would I do, with no college education?

I walked back into our home and looked at all the now-empty rooms, and I sat on the stairs and cried my eyes out, feeling very, very alone. It was here, though, on those stairs, that I began to feel helped, guided, protected. I began to sense a presence within me, an energy of support around me. It was very subtle, but somehow, I knew that I was not alone. Again, I just had a knowing that someone was with me. It gave me a calmness, just as it did when I was a young girl in my room, trying to sleep.

It was very soon after this that things began to shift.

I decided to become a photographer one day, just like that. It was not something I always wanted to do or try; I just thought it would be great for me to do as a job since I could make my own hours and be available for my kids. I borrowed money to buy a camera and was gifted a beautiful lens from a special friend who believed in me and to whom I will always be grateful. My mother helped me with daycare, and I managed to muster the courage to just go for it.

Again, my ex-husband said I was crazy, a terrible photographer. That I "couldn't correctly frame a picture if I tried." I had no experience, no training, no benevolent mentor to show me the ropes. So, I just created my own educational program. In a way, he was right. I didn't know how to be a photographer. Yet I flourished in the industry. I created a business that brought a lot of happiness to families. I took beautiful photographs of children. I became a well-known children's photographer. Things lined up; big opportunities presented themselves to me. Whenever I was short of money as I was building my business, money just came to me like magic. It could be a day of new clients or a refund check showing up in the mail with almost the exact amount of money I needed. I kept being guided down this career path. I paid attention, and one opportunity led to another. Before I knew it, I was supporting myself and my kids. I worked hard, and business kept coming my way. I traveled all over the United States, and clients came to me from other countries. Life had a flow, and I felt I was swimming with it. I knew that I could be successful if I listened to myself. I look back now on that career, and it was absolutely training for my mediumship development.

My next major spiritual experience was ten years later, when my ex-husband passed away. On the second day after he passed, my phone rang. It was for my younger son, and as I called for him and waited for him to pick up the phone from the other room, I stayed on the receiver. Once he was on the line, I started to hang up, but I heard this loud static coming from the phone. As my son's conversation continued in the background, I heard my ex-husband's voice coming through the static. Every hair on my arms stood up, and I froze in shock. He was talking to our son, who clearly couldn't hear him. But I could.

The next night, I laid in bed, trying to sleep, fretting over the boys' emotional states after losing their father. It was about one in the morning when I noticed an electric blue light bobbing above my bedroom door. For some reason, I was compelled to speak to it. Just as I finished, I had the strong sensation of someone next to me. Through my shock, I turned and was overwhelmed by the feeling of being embraced and felt the brush of a hand on my own. I'll never forget the unexpected sense of comfort I received, like a gift.

The experiences kept coming. I heard someone say hello to me from thin air when I went into a powder room one day. I woke in the middle of the night and went downstairs to lay on the couch, and someone sat down on the couch right next to me, and the cushion actually moved. I began to feel a subtle energy around me like a sort of surging light frequency as I was doing mundane things such as the dishes or driving. I had a recurring spiritual dream that was so vivid I could not stop thinking about it for days afterward.

Come January 2016, it was a new year and a time for new resolutions. I decided to start meditating. About three weeks in, things really began to unfold. I would be walking my dog and would receive downloads of information, like a block of thought, put into my brain. One morning I heard a voice urging me to "listen to Calvin Harris and think of her." Though I didn't have many songs of *that artist, I did have a single song on my playlist titled "I Feel So Close to You."*

One afternoon, I attended a guided meditation during which you were urged to set an intention to connect with whomever you desired. I knew that I wanted to see my spirit guide. Toward the end of the meditation, she appeared with an incredible flash of vision so clear, sharp, bright, and big, it was unmistakable. Here was my guide, finally!

She sat on a bench, dressed in white, her long, dark hair loosely up in a bun. The setting was outdoors, in the country, and she had a soft smile. As this vision proceeded, an overwhelming feeling of absolute love washed over me. Now, when she comes through in readings, she always starts by identifying herself this way, though she will at times also appear with the man in the hat from my childhood. The last song I'd heard in my car before I pulled up to go to that meditation was the Calvin Harris number; and after that—I kid you not—that song was always the last to play whenever I would go to do my mediumship work as I was developing. It was her way of letting me know she's there, I suppose.

Spirit started to show up in the middle of the night, giving me downloads, images, and messages. I learned to ask who was speaking, and this helped a great deal, as I would then receive names, descriptions, or other helpful information. This went on for months. Sometimes I knew them and other times I did not. There were nights this went on for several hours as I tried to sleep. It was not the spirits that pushed me to understand all that was happening, but rather the incredible strength of energy I sometimes felt. Often, it was strong, like electricity, and would wake me from a deep sleep. This was a very different feeling from loved ones in spirit stopping by to visit. It really got my attention, which I think was the point. I would run out of my bedroom a little scared of this intense energy that kept showing up. What was it?

It was this search for answers that led me straight to mediumship. Clearly, this resonated with my experiences, and I needed to learn how to deal with it and understand its purpose in my life.

Then came an evening in January 2017, and I was settling into bed for the night. I became comfortable and relaxed, and again I received that surge of energy around me. It was a force so intense, so obvious it could not be overlooked or brushed aside. I had been working very hard in developing my mediumistic skills and had learned to communicate very well with spirit. So when this energy came to me again, I found the courage to ask who it was. The reply floored me. I was told that this energy or being was to be my mentor and that the time had come for me to know him. The energy then receded, leaving me to try to understand what this was going to mean for me.

I awoke at five the next morning to find a rather Egyptian-looking fellow at the foot of my bed. His eyes captivated me. In fact, I could not stop staring at them. He was gentle but exuded an aura of authority and gravity—the demeanor of an important man. Finally, I looked away and got out of bed, and by the time I looked back, he was gone.

I had an urge to start writing that morning. I decided to try automatic writing. Inspired writing. I had tried in the past with complete frustration, but that morning, I felt differently. After a brief meditation, I took a few deep breaths and sat with my pen and paper. Within a few moments, I began to get first impressions, visions, and downloads, which turned into words; and I began to write. It went in fits and starts at first—sometimes just a word or short sentence—until the words started to flow from my hand like water from a pitcher. I didn't think, didn't stop, didn't know what was coming. I was just there as the thoughts unfolded onto the paper. It was amazing! I was communicating with my guides.

We did these writings in the morning for nine months, off and on. What started with pen and paper continued over onto the computer. The flow of information grew; the level of communication became stronger. A dialogue began. I would ask a question, and they would joyfully answer. I learned their personalities. I felt their love. I enjoyed their humor. I learned who they were and how many they were. They taught me things about spiritual growth, what I was to do in my life, why they were with me, how they each help me, and so on.

At the end of this nine months with them, I again awoke one morning with an urge. It seems they always impress an urge upon me when they want me to do something. I think it's my idea, but really, it's probably theirs.

Alas, they can see my life path a bit better from their vantage point so it's nice that they let me think this, even if only for a little while. This time, I had the urge to write a book.

This was our dialogue:

September 07, 2017

Good morning,

I have a desire to share an idea with you and would like your thoughts on it. I would like to write a book with you. You have so much wisdom and have been great teachers, and we can share this with so many. How do you feel about this? Would you enjoy doing this with me?

Good morning to you, my dear. It is a day starting off with much inspiration. This is very nice, indeed. You speak of a book. We say books are a wonderful way to bring wisdom and knowledge to those who seek it. It is a good idea. We do this with you in a similar way already, so to create this book will just take some daily discipline from you to sit each day with us to produce the needed material. We say we can do this with you, and it will be quite fun. We shall do this each day. We can start with supplying you with set "need" topics, and see how it unfolds and develops. We would wish this to be an easy read. A book that can be enjoyed and looked back on several times for the reader. A book where, each time a page is revisited, it shares additional knowledge that can help the readers along their journey. What a wonderful process to take part in. You can use your abilities in such a way that can brighten the lives of others. It is light workers at their best. We see this as a passion project that can and will give much to many and to those everywhere who seek the information. We shall reflect on topics that are of interest to many. It can point them to the paths their souls' and hearts' desire.

Let us meet up as we do in meditation each day at the same time and with a start and finish date, yes? We enjoy very much to have this opportunity with you and to put you on your path as well, you see. To start you on your course, let us begin this passion project with a desire and intention to help those seeking and who need the wisdom and knowledge we can offer. We say let us go for this in full force and begin this project each day at 7:30. We can write each day for forty minutes and no longer. Keep your writings organized and detailed and structured in such a way that transcripts can be presented easily, you see. Thank you for the time together. We enjoy working with you, as this is our desire to be with you and to move you up to your best, and to also shine your light for all to see. It is a fine time.

We shall connect again soon, and we shall be ready and excited for this time. Be well, and know we are here and are excited and have great love for you always.

Each morning, I welcomed them in with a few minutes of breathing in and out and setting the intention to work, as laid out.

As I sit and reflect back on the incredible journey that has unfolded for me during these past few years, I cannot help but see the changes in myself. I am noticing all the things

I have learned about myself, the unique qualities I have found within myself and all the happiness I have created for myself by seeing and living life differently through the help, wisdom, and love of my spirit guides. This has been the road trip of a lifetime. My heart is full of appreciation because I have learned from them how to navigate to the roads where I can feel my joy, understand and live with purpose, and create more of what I want to come into my experience each day.

Acknowledgments

I have many people to thank for all that has happened, and I would like to start first by thanking my guides. Thank you from the bottom of my heart. You are my very beautiful spirit dream team, and I love you, and I have tremendous appreciation for you. You have been my loudest cheerleaders, my biggest supporters, and my greatest teachers. To know you has changed my life. You taught me how to find me, to really know and feel who I am and what I am here to do in life. I sit in absolute gratitude every day to feel your presence around me and to have the ability to connect and to share your teachings with all who read this book.

To my incredible husband, Joe, who has been on quite the ride with me. Your love, support, and faith in me have never faltered.

You have trusted me and have openly and willingly taken in all my many incredible spiritual experiences that have gone on to become the new normal in our life with such ease. My hope is I have enhanced your life with the same care and love with which you have consistently enhanced mine. I love you.

My children, Kyle and Cole, you have been source for everything I do. You are my absolute heart. My greatest accomplishment in life will always be being a mother to both of you. I love you to the moon and back.

To Lorri Walker, thank you for getting me walking on my spiritual path. I believe from the bottom of my heart that I was guided to you. You lit the way for me, and you will always be a bright light in my life.

To my late father, who showed me by example how to have a good work ethic. I am very grateful for that. He always believed in me, and that gave me great confidence to persevere through the challenges life presented me. I love you Dad.

To my beautiful mother, who showed me incredible strength in life. I learned from her to be strong. I could always count on her, and there were days I needed that. She never disappointed. I love you Mom.

To my clients, you have truly opened my heart. I thank you for trusting me and being vulnerable and open with your emotions during our sessions together. Our readings together showed me that so many needed some help finding their happiness. That many yearned for a life filled with purpose and passion. That after losing a loved one, so many lost their way a bit and wanted to get back to life and find joy again but struggled with how to do it. Your stories inspired me. Your pain and sadness from a loss of a loved one motivated me. I want to help people who need it get their groove back and to discover themselves, to feel good and to find that happiness from within. My hope is you can find some inspiration in this book to lean on and to practice the teachings whenever you need it.

In love and light,
Monica

Introduction

*Get to know the beauty of
yourself, what truly moves
you and inspires you.*

Spirituality is a word with different meanings to different people. This book is not here to tell you what spirituality is or should be to you but rather for you to discover for yourself what it is and means for you. It is a place within you, a sacred place where discoveries of yourself can and will be awoken.

We are not trying to say that you are asleep, only that life can turn down your personal awareness. It causes you to become distracted from who you really are and more focused on what is going on outside of you.

To remember who you are, try to spend less time on things around you and more time on yourself. Get to know the beauty of yourself, what truly moves you and inspires you. Feel what desires sit within you. This is what we would like you to awaken yourself to. This is exactly why spirituality means different things to different people. Within oneself resides one's very own unique beauty and the incredible desires that move and inspire one to take action and draw to one the very things one wishes to experience.

Through this book, we wish to get you thinking of those things that move you. To begin to awaken yourself to that absolute beauty that sits within you. To become aware of yourself and to truly get to know who you really are.

The purpose here is to share easy, practical ways to find yourself and put you on a path of joy and of happiness. We believe that when you know yourself and begin to see the magnificence that you are and the possibilities that are there for you and all the incredible desires that sit idle within you, you will begin to find your power, your calling, your happiness. You'll find your innate ability to create the life you want with the joy that you deserve. This is our passion project: to help you become all that you are made to be; to be able to see yourself for all that you are, can be, and are meant to be.

We wish that you see the pages that await you as a marvelous treasure chest of jewels, filled with all sorts of beautiful and vibrant gems. These gems are *you*.

This is meant to be an easy process, for we wish this journey of self-discovery to be fun and light. We want to create simple steps for you to shine your light bright.

We hope to help you find what brings you joy, happiness, and fulfillment in all areas of your life. We say it is all there within you. It really is nothing that needs to be created; it merely needs to be *found* within you. Allow us to help you on your path and give you the map you need on this journey to find yourself and your own personal spirituality. It is different for everyone, and isn't that wonderful?

Who We Are

We are oneness. We are us, and we are you. We are a bit of all that is here, and you are as well.

Before we go any further, we want you to understand who we are. For you to truly understand this book and the purpose behind this passion project, we want very much for you to know us. We are energy, first and foremost. We are within all things, and, yes, this means things that are around you. We are individuals and also a collective

1

group. We choose at any time how we like to step forward. We are here, for the purpose of this book, as a collective group. We are here to share with you wonderful ways of being you! We are teachers. We are helpers.

We are here to help you connect with your innate wants, wishes, and desires. We are here to come together and be of service to you and to help you along on your life journey. It is our absolute wish to have all of you find happiness, joy, and purpose. This means different things to different individuals, yet we know that the words we express here will help you in the exact way you need. We are guides; yes, this is true. We have been here with Monica for her entire life. It has been our desire to have this time together, to be a part of this project, and to be of help and guidance to those who seek it. We are a oneness. We are us, and we are you. We are a bit of all that is here, and you are as well.

We come to you with great love. It is our intention to add to your life a new way of seeing yourself—the *correct* way of seeing yourself. The *only* way of seeing yourself. This way is with absolute love. So we come forward now at this time because it is the right time. The desire and need are supercharged.

When the desire and need create this level of energy, it is our wanting to direct this energy and have it flow toward and through *you* to achieve an open and receptive state of love. For yourself, yes, but also for others.

When we are together—we meaning this group writing these words for you—we want you to understand and feel that the power of such a collective group, with such a desire to serve you and your potential, brings forth incredible possibilities. This power sits within you as well. We are here to be of value to you, to help you be all you can and to do all you are meant to do. To find your purpose, your heart's greatest desire.

We are Edgar, and we love you.

We want you to soar through life with confidence and know that your wings are strong and that you can be all you wish to be. This is different for each of you, and we understand that not all have the same needs and desires. (How dull that would be!) We do know, however, that each of you can benefit from the teachings we wish to share. They can help you experience this life with incredible joy.

We are many here, and we give you our name as singular for it is just easier this way.

Know that we are a group that wants to share ways that we see from our place that can and will be of benefit to you. For as you apply the things we speak of, you will feel lighter and more joyful. When you can connect with your true self, this is how you will feel.

We are excited for this process and for this time and place—this now—to be able to bring forward our knowledge and our absolute love for you.

So let us begin.

Who You Are

The light within you is you. It is all you really are. Tap into the light.

✧ ✧ ✧

To know that you are here now, reading these words and turning each page, is to know you are ready and desire this information. It's possible you have felt stuck or uncertain of yourself. We understand that you have been searching for something, for a sign that says, "Go this way!" We want you to know that you are correct in looking for the signs. They are there. Each and every day, these signs are presenting themselves to you from your soul— from your true self, your best and highest self. You see, it knows you. Yes, it is true. It knows you very well, better than you know yourself at this moment and those that came before. To look for the signs is not wrong. It is, in fact, quite right. You have a system within you—a very strong, smart system—that runs you. It runs you like a powerful engine should. Each day, your soul is speaking to you. Each day, your soul is crying out for you to listen. Each day, your soul is wanting to make your life beautiful, to make your life full and filled with joy. To know your soul is the most important step toward all you wish to be.

We ask you, "Do you even know what it is that you want?" There are days you may sit and ponder this question, days you maybe even feel you know. Yet, are you happy? Are you experiencing the things that create the life, the joy, and the love that you wish to have? Do you understand yourself?

We are here to share with you beautiful ways to discover yourself. To create the life you want, to have the experiences you want, and to enjoy a life you really want, you must know what you want. You must *feel* what you want. You must see the signs that draw you toward and onto the path that brings you what you want. What happens, however, is doubt: the unsure feeling of not understanding yourself. Not knowing yourself. The true you. The deeper you. The all-knowing you. The beautiful you.

Your soul knows. It knows with absolute certainty what you love, what you enjoy, and what brings you happiness and fulfillment. It knows your path. It knows your future and your purpose. It knows it all. It is not something you must make or create. It is already there for you. Your deepest, truest heart's desire is already within you. It is *your* soul. Trust it.

It is there. Why are you not seeing it? Why are you not feeling it, enjoying it? That light from within that is so bright that it shines outward to the world to touch not only you but your family, your friends, your coworkers, and your community. That light sits inside you. The light within you *is* you. It is all that you really are. Tap into that light. It is filled with those feelings you desire to have each and every day. It is happiness, joy, and love made to manifest. That light holds everything you are, including all your talents, desires, hopes, and dreams. It holds you at your fullest, *and* it contains your personal map to get you everywhere you are meant to go and to be.

This light tries each day to give you signs to point you in the right direction to all you really want. That light is never wrong, off, or in error. It holds all your abilities and knows where they should be directed. It knows your possibilities, and we promise there are many. Get to know yourself. It is the absolute best relationship you can ever have.

So many of you spend so much time trying to get to know new friends and pursuing new romantic relationships, but do you put the same effort in knowing *yourself?* Allow yourself to know yourself. You will love yourself once you feel everything you really are. It is a love so big and so deep. Love yourself first.

Once you develop this relationship, it will not disappoint, for from this place of knowing who you are and all that you can do and be, magic unfolds. The beauty, the light, can be seen and can shine as it is meant to. So begin by looking within. Allow us to help you meet yourself. Allow us to introduce you to your soul.

Exercise: The Starting Point

It is not a coincidence that you are reading this book at this time. This book was put in your path by your need and desire for change and as one of those signs we just talked about. The questions for you are: What brought you here? What made you decide to pick up this book and start reading it at this particular time?

Spend some time reflecting on:

- Who you are
- What you are about
- What is important to you
- Where you think your life is going
- How you feel
- What you would like to do differently
- How all this led to this very moment

Write this down so that you can later see what your starting point was for this incredible journey ahead.

CHAPTER

3

Know Where You Are Headed

✧ ✧ ✧

You must begin to know how you want to be changed by the experiences you will have.

✧ ✧ ✧

Here you are. You are ready to go. The car is fueled, and the luggage is packed. You sit in the car, ready to go toward all that can be, but where are you going? What does it look like? What does it feel like? What does it mean to you? Is this a trip you have always wanted to take? Are you going for good weather? Are you going for the culture? The food? The people? One must know a bit about where one wants to go in order to put foot to pedal and actually *go*.

When you plan a vacation, you know what you want from that vacation. You know that you want relaxation or culture or beautiful, peaceful scenery or good weather or adventure. You have an itinerary. You know exactly what you want to experience. We say it is the same here and now. Treat this journey to self the same as you would when planning a vacation. Just allowing yourself to begin to think and *feel* about where you want to go will give you the biggest clues to your destination.

Now, you can and will come across parts of the journey that feel uninteresting, perhaps like miles of desert that have nothing to see for hours but cactus. There's nothing to draw your attention, nothing to focus on, and you might find yourself feeling a bit dull for this piece of the ride. It can be that you are discovering the lack of passion within yourself during this part of the trip. It can also be that weather conditions can surface that are unexpected and catch you unprepared, such as a rainstorm, snowstorm, or windstorm. There can be parts of this journey where you become emotional or vulnerable, and there could be tears as you begin driving through these parts of the trip.

But sometimes the view of this road will be absolutely magnificent, the stops along the way filled with excitement. And in these moments, you can sit back and enjoy the challenges that brought you here.

You must begin to know how you want to be changed by the experiences you will have. That is where you must begin. Get in the car, have a place in mind, and turn on the motor and start driving.

Exercise: The Destination

Think about times in your life when you felt connected, blissful, safe, at peace. Think about how things worked out for you. Think about how your relationships worked well and how life unfolded for you with much greater ease. What made you happy? What things moved you, inspired you, uplifted you?

Write down every positive thing you can think of when you remember these moments—every aspect, no matter how insignificant they seem. If it made you feel good, it was not insignificant!

Intentions

*The word is a word only until one
puts the essence of one's desires into it.*

Now you are on your way. You have left the driveway and have entered the highway. As you move along, there is something we wish to discuss: intentions. We say this and know many of you have heard of this word before. What does it mean to you?

Intentions are a powerful force. They are your direct communication to all the power that sits within the universe. A word is a word only until you put the essence of your desire into it. Then it becomes something much more. Any new project, any new process, and any new focus should be built on a solid structure of intentions. To improve in a certain area, one must put power toward it. One must be able to feed that desire. Setting intentions is a way to do this.

So, how do you set an intention that will be the correct structure for building upon? Look into your heart. Quite simply, ask. Put your desires and hopes out there. This is not praying or dreaming. There is a system for intention, a way it is meant to be created and used, a way it should look and feel.

Remember what we said about finding your joy? You're going to need it here! You must find your heart's truest desire, your purest joy, in order to find your calling. And this is where your passion comes into play—a deep wanting of the work. Each day, you must set your intentions of what you wish to do, make, have, build, or experience.

But intention isn't enough. One must also have the *passion* and put the energy toward, the intention. Intention + passion = creation. It cannot happen any other way. It is only through the correct application of this formula that you will really begin to create your destination.

Your intention is the solid structure upon which you can build your dream and make it a reality. To have something you want, you must feel into what you want. Start each day by pulling forward the power that is there for you.

Do not just say what you want; you must also *feel* what you want. The feeling is what draws to you the power to help you achieve your goals. You have incredible support around you. Begin to reach for it. Setting intentions allows you to begin tapping into the enormous support system that sits around, waiting for you to request its help. It is there. Make no mistake of it. It is loving you and wanting to support you.

We say this is the first piece to having all you desire. It is to cry out to your soul for what you want most from the deepest of your heart. Intentions reside within the heart. Your passion will fuel their manifestations.

Exercise: Intend!

Find a quiet, safe space—one that is welcoming, where no focus needs to be given to anything but the work you're about to do.

Now, sit quietly each day for a few minutes in this space and take some breaths in and out. Then drop your mind toward your heart (imagine this). And then from that heart space, set out your intentions. You can say your intentions out loud or in your mind; it makes no difference at all. Do whatever you are comfortable with.

Put as much feeling as possible into your intentions. How will their manifestation feel to you? What will it mean to you? How will it move you? Is it a feeling of love, happiness, peace, joy? Dwell on that feeling. Sit with that feeling and allow it to move you from inside.

This is a start of giving to yourself. This also allows you to be present with yourself, your soul, your heart. Enjoy the feeling, the exercise, and the start toward creating that power within and around you.

Begin now.

Gratitude

*Gratitude is not hard to feel
if you open your heart.*

There are several very important structures that are key to having happiness, finding one's true self, and having the life that one desires and deserves. These structures are important for building on the foundation of oneself. To be strong and solid within, one must also be willing to look outside of oneself.

There is another very important word, and it has been spoken of by many, but it is a word we feel few have a true understanding of. This word is *gratitude*. We say the word here, and as we say it, we wish you to feel this word and think what it means to you. How does it fit in your life? *Is* it in your life? Do you call upon it on any given day? Do you understand the feeling within this word?

As we say it now, we feel immense love toward you, for we are so grateful you are taking the time to read this book and truly think and feel the words we express for you here. We are grateful, yes.

The word *gratitude* is a word of love. It *is* love. It is a very high vibration word. And when you apply it to your life, miracles happen, doors open, opportunities present themselves, Mr. or Mrs. Right walks into your life, a career enhances, and pregnancies can happen when you have wished for a baby.

Gratitude is you lining yourself up with the power of love. Did you ever hear this word and understand that its meaning was love? We wish you to begin feeling and connecting with this word, *gratitude*. We say it is so easy to do, and yet so many do not do it. So much of people's days are spent in the "without" mind set. The "I don't have enough" mindset, the "I wish I had this" or "I wish I could go there" mindset. We wish to explain to you that you cannot get to any of those places with that mindset. We are sorry, but it cannot be. *To be, do, and have all your heart wants, you must start from already seeing what you have.* Be grateful for the things that *have* gone right, for the opportunities that *did* work out, for the places you *have* been.

You see, it is not possible to go from a feeling of lack to a feeling of fulfillment with a mindset that is empty of gratitude. So, what does the word *really* mean? Gratitude, as we said, is love. And *love* is the most powerful word in existence. When applied correctly, it can transform lives. So, understand that gratitude must be in your structure of becoming everything you want and have and do. The energy of gratitude must be within your personal energy, and it is like a rocket. It is so fast and so powerful that it can take you anywhere, no matter how far it may feel for you in the moment. It is there and available for you to work with. In fact, it is waiting to be acknowledged. It is waiting to be understood and used correctly so it can take off toward all you wish. Without it, you will be far slower to arrive at your destination.

Gratitude is being appreciative and thankful for what you have. Gratitude is not hard to feel if you open your heart. One may say, "I have nothing to be grateful for," and here we giggle because there is so much to be grateful for. If you find yourself feeling very depleted by life, if it has given you hard knocks, you can begin with the basics of being grateful—any little thing you can think of. So many of you take for granted the basics that, at the end of the day, are the most important things. When you bypass these gifts that you have and overlook them, it slows down your vibration. We say be grateful for what you have, what is working for you, what opportunities you do have, the home you are in—and this goes on and on.

Begin turning around the way you see things in your life. Stand each day in appreciation and gratefulness for all that has worked out for you. When you turn your mindset away from the lack and toward the gifts, you will change within you your very own vibration frequency. This vibration within you will begin to rise. When the vibration rises, you will be very aware because you will feel happier. You will have more smiles and a bit of a bounce beneath your feet as you step out into the world. As you stay focused on this grateful mindset, you will begin to see and feel shifts within you, and you will begin attracting more of the same feelings through new experiences and opportunities. And again more vibration within will rise, and you will begin to expand yourself and your soul to the very things you want: joy, love, wealth, happiness, relationships, and absolutely anything else. You will get it all, you see. We promise you, when you live with gratitude, it becomes a life well lived.

Exercise: Cultivating Gratitude

Make yourself a checklist, sorted by category, be it relationships, career, personal life, finances, home, health, etc. What are you grateful for in each category? Write this in your sectioned categories. What has worked out for you? What hidden aspects or opportunities for gratitude lie within these neat little categories you've made? Identify three things, at a very minimum, that you are grateful for.

Now, sit each day and start off with these three thoughts of gratitude. For at least a few minutes, sit with these thoughts and allow those thoughts to create emotion within you. Recall the way your body felt, and let that feeling wash over you now as you feel each area you feel thankful for and your gratitude toward each item from each category.

Once you have gotten comfortable with this, pick another three things. Feel the beauty in these events. *Search* for the hidden gems, the less obvious. Each time you sit, more thoughts of gratitude will emerge and more categories will appear. Soon you will not only see but also feel the quantity of things within your life you can be and feel grateful for.

Extra credit:

There also is great spiritual value for you to create a list of things that occurred that were challenging, difficult, or emotional. Things that have happened to you that may have been difficult but made you grow. Beauty can be found in every experience. Feel those experiences and search for the good in those times. Feel a sense of their purpose for showing up in your life. They brought value to you—know this. Sit and be grateful within this area of yourself also, for these circumstances shaped you.

Meditation

*To know yourself, you
must sit with yourself.*

This next piece of your personal journey to self is an important one. They are all important, but this one holds with it a need for you to be available. To be available for yourself, for this practice, is for you and you alone. This is your time. When you implement it for yourself, you will know yourself. We speak of meditation.

Meditation is a word you all have heard. Some of you might think it is for the spiritual/

New Age crowd, or people who are into yoga, and indeed, people who enjoy those things may meditate. But we want you to see that meditation is for everyone. Meditation can be a practice for all, even children. Yes, it is true. *To know yourself, you must sit with yourself.* Meditation is where you can do this. One may ask, "How do I get to know myself by saying and doing nothing?" We say that much is said in meditation. Much is dealt with and worked on in meditation. Words are not needed to get to know yourself. It is a time to feel, and it is those feelings that allow you to know yourself. It is the calmness that allows you to hear yourself. There are no words needed to get to know the real you. The true you. The all that is you. Isn't it wonderful to be able to sit and simply be with yourself and know you are accomplishing much?

We know so many of you work to accomplish much, do much, in each day. Perhaps you feel pressure and stress engulf your life from all the demands. Deadlines. Accomplishments. The endless day-to-day routines. We understand the need, the push to get things done. Work responsibilities require much from you. That family can carry many responsibilities. We understand this. But do you see that you go and go and go and go, and at times you feel as though you cannot stop, shut off, wind down? You go from one project to another responsibility to the next routine to the next goal to the next, next, next. Your days and weeks and months are much this way. Packed with noise. Packed with things that don't give you joy. Packed with things that take and don't give much back. Many of you feel depleted. Tired. Run down. Even hopeless that you'll never be able to get off the ride. If this is true for you, you have created a life on auto-pilot. You are that machine that never shuts down. We want you to understand, if you don't even shut down for maintenance, the machine that is you will *break down.*

There is a tremendous value in recharging, in allowing yourself to shut down for a little bit. Meditation does this. Meditation is where you get to know your soul, your true self, the highest form of you. The all that you are. You are brilliant. You are capable of most anything your heart desires. To connect with yourself in this most wonderful way allows you to connect with all you are, all you want, all you need. We understand some ask, "How can I connect with myself by just sitting in a chair and being quiet?"

Well, much growth happens in meditation. Correction: *very much* growth happens in meditation. Be on your road to self. To take this trip of self-discovery, there must be meditation. It is opening yourself up. It is allowing you to see your own light, those talents and passions that lay dormant.

As you meditate, you are with yourself, your soul. As you connect with your soul, it is not possible to not be happy. It is not. As you incorporate this practice into your life, your life will get an energy boost. You will start to feel more energetic, happier, calmer. Things that once bothered you become a bit less bothersome. You begin to see life and all the things in it differently. We call this *awareness*. What a word. A wonderful word. To be aware of you, your life, and all that's in it is to change the color of it all. It becomes brighter and more vibrant.

We wish to also say that when you begin your practice, you will experience much. You will, from time to time, feel things you have not felt in perhaps many years. This may be not while meditating but perhaps afterward. As you sit within yourself, some feelings may have you experience tears. This is perfect. Sitting in your practice of meditation and increasing your awareness is much like cleaning out the closet, you see. You may find things within you that no longer serve you.

We say it is time to spring clean. Clear out the closets. We must make room for the new stuff, the good stuff, the bigger and better stuff, the all you are to become.

Certainly, when you take on the project of spring cleaning, it is a project you most likely have put off often. It is a chore many do not wish to spend their time doing. When working within yourself, this will be true also. Just be aware that it is all good. Room must be made. Why? Because it's hard to create in tons of clutter.

As you meditate, some days will feel euphoric and some days not. Some days, you may feel nothing shifting at all. *We say, much work is being done. Much is happening for the self.* When you meditate, you may possibly have feelings and sensations. Some of these sensations, movements, and feelings can be as follows: Tingling on the scalp, numbness in the limbs, feeling of heat or cold, a breeze around you, a feeling of floating, and perhaps an arm moves or twitches. These are just some examples of what one may experience during meditations. It is very good.

Allow it to occur. It is you changing vibration. These experiences may happen more in the beginning of your practice because once your body adjusts to a higher vibration, it will have fewer of those experiences. You may also feel head movement. Your head may go right, left, or move circular. It is also possible that you could lean in one direction. Any of these are also very good, for this is your body loosening up that junk in the closets, you see. It's making way to remove the unwanted stuff. These are all things that could happen. You may not experience any of these or you may experience only a few, but we wish you to understand what it is if it happens. It is all very good.

To really know yourself and begin to feel all that is there for you, you must sit. You must sit and be still. Be quiet. There is much to learn in the silence. Many have a misunderstanding of meditation. Many have tried it and felt they could not do it.

"It was hard. I could not get mind to stop thinking."

"I am not meant to meditate."

"I have too much energy."

"I am a type-A personality."

"I meditate in other ways."

"I don't know what kind of meditation to do."

Sound familiar? We understand when you say you have tried and you have struggled. It is not that you are not able, your personality is not meant for meditation, or that your mind is too busy. You can, and we will share now with you how to do it. We wish you to have all that you want. We wish you to be all you can be. We wish you to know yourself for the absolute love that you are, the incredible gift that you truly are to the world. Be patient with yourself, and we ask you now to try it our way.

Now to begin this practice, we say you should try your very best to meditate the same time each day. Treat it much the same way as an appointment you make. If you can do this every day, this is wonderful. If you can do this just a few times a week, then this is also good. If possible, do your meditation practice daily and at the same time, for your benefits will be massive. Find a time and a space that is quiet and not active. Find a time and place each day that will be uninterrupted. Turn off phones and find a place that feels good to do your practice. Start your practice with just ten minutes to warm up the engines, and get a feeling for yourself and a rhythm within you moving.

We would enjoy seeing you sit for thirty minutes daily, so add five minutes each month toward your sitting time as a process to grow your practice (or sooner, if you feel ready) until you reach thirty minutes. Before you begin any practice, be sure you have first been seen and approved to do so by your physician. The process to meditate well is to sit comfortably: legs crossed or legs touching the ground, shoulder-width apart. Whatever inspires you. Do not lay down as this can make you fall asleep. Hands in your lap. We wish to say that we know that many say they cannot get thoughts away and they enter often. This is okay. It is not possible to not have thoughts ever. As your practice improves, less thoughts will surface, but they will still surface. We say to you to allow the thought to enter and then move it aside. Do not give it any attention. Acknowledge the thought and then instantly brush it to the side and go back to feeling your breath. To meditate, you do want an active mind, otherwise you may fall asleep. We wish the mind to be active, but the purpose is to be aware: aware of your surroundings, aware of any sensations. *Aware but not a participant in what is around you.* Do you see the difference?

Exercise: Relax. It's Meditation

Go into your practice expecting nothing. Expect no communication. Expect no inspiration. Nothing. It is to just be with yourself. Sit comfortably. Envision yourself still, and sit a moment with that vision as your body adjusts to the position. Then begin breathing. One deep breath in, and one deep breath out. Follow your breath. If you can put your attention to your breath and feel and follow the breath go into the body and out of the body, this is very helpful. It allows your mind to have something to do, you see. If a thought enters, simply acknowledge it and put it aside. Give it no attention. Be aware of the thought and then push it away and go back to your breathing. This will happen many times throughout the meditation, and it is fine. After you have taken several deep breaths and your shoulders have fallen a bit and you feel a sense of relaxation in the body, continue breathing in and out, a bit less deep than before and only what feels comfortable to you. Once your body feels more relaxed, with your next breath we would like you to breathe in, but as you exhale, we wish you to take your breath to the heart area. Again allow your mind to follow the breath to the heart area. Breathe into the heart area, keeping your mind on the in breath and out breath. After several breaths this way and a few moments spent here, begin to breathe in and out again. With the next out breath, drop your breath into the stomach area, the solar plexus. We wish you now to stay there with your mind and with your breath. Your breath will have found its own rhythm. Feel this area.

Welcome to your soul.

Stay here for the remainder of your practice time. Time will go quickly. Do not be surprised if you are excited for your next session with yourself.

As you build upon this practice and add minutes spent in your soul, you will be providing yourself the best gift you could ever offer to yourself. And that gift is *you*.

Congratulations!

CHAPTER

7

Thoughts and Energy

Thoughts are the start of all things.

Thoughts enter the mind every day, all day. You are all the same in this way. As much as you may not want to believe it, thoughts drive your every emotion. Negative thoughts turn into uncomfortable emotions, and positive ones in *up* or happy emotions.

Thoughts are not something you can *avoid.* The type of thoughts you hold within your mind can carry with them emotions that can feel good or not. What we wish you to understand is that it is key to your happiness to be aware of each thought that you have. You can learn to be aware of your thoughts. It is a similar practice to what we suggested while meditating, only you do it while you are going through your day. It is a way to be mindful of yourself and the thoughts that surround your life.

You will have thoughts; you will have thousands of them each day. However, not all thoughts carry feelings with them. Some drop in and out, barely a blip on the emotional radar. It is the thoughts that *do* carry the emotions along with them that we wish you to become aware of and change if the emotions associated with them are not emotions you *wish* to feel. If the thought makes you feel uneasy, uncomfortable, worried, frightened, insecure, and so on. It is thoughts with emotions like these attached to them that serve you no good. None at all. If these enter your mind, they also must leave your mind. You need to create an exit door for all thoughts that do not serve you or your best and highest good, and you must start thinking this way.

If you fill your mind with thoughts that are not empowering, they will fill your being with more thoughts associated with similar feelings, and before you know it, you are having one very bad day. It doesn't have to be this way. You *can* choose. We want to express to you that every thought has a feeling toward it, on a scale of low to high. The strength of the thought and the association you create for yourself will determine the emotions you have with the thought. You will have thoughts, yes. And it won't always feel like you have control of them. But we want you to understand the power you have toward them. No thought can make you feel any way unless you allow it.

Learn to be a trainer of your own thoughts. Reward the good thoughts by feeling them, *being* them. Starve the bad thoughts by starving them out. When a bad or negative thought comes in, you acknowledge it, give no emotion or feeling toward it, and push it away. Allow it to go hungry.

Thoughts are so important because energy flows where attention goes. Source energy is constantly moving through the world in which you live. It is a power source that supports each and every one of you. It is forever moving and flowing throughout each and every thing within your existence. It is in each breath that you take in each moment.

It is part of each thing you touch and each thought you have. It is the breeze on your face. *Its purpose is to create.* It is a massive artist, and it can help you if you understand the way it flows and moves with life.

This energy source can do so much for you when directed correctly. Its intention is to put more of itself toward any and all things that it is drawn toward. It is always creating, and so what you are thinking about and what you choose to put your attention upon allows this energy to work. Your intentions and your desires are like a paintbrush and paint to this energy, and with a large canvas being life, it begins painting a bit more onto it each day.

The more time you spend having inspiring thoughts, and the more you experience heartfelt desires and thoughts within you, the quicker this energy moves. By this action, and with more of these thoughts, more paint strokes are placed onto this canvas. It is creating everything you put your attention to. It can paint you a masterpiece, and it can paint you a scribble. It accelerates when its focus draws closer and closer to something, and it can create something remarkable in what seems like an instant.

Source energy has incredible power, and it attracts itself and moves toward that which is strongest, whether that be happy thoughts or fearful thoughts. It is not particular and gives you more of what it gets, so negative becomes *more* negative and positive becomes *more* positive. A bad hour becomes and bad day, which can become a bad week.

Everything begins as a thought. There must first be the idea of anything at all before the creation of anything at all. It is all thought first. Everything. Think of it as a magnificent pool of possibilities for the energy to draw toward and to create with. You each create your very own pool of thoughts. Energy goes toward the thoughts that have the most strength. It is pulled toward that which draws it near.

You are in charge; you must know this. You must be aware at all times of what you put into your mind. Be aware of what your thoughts are and what they feel like to you. Choose thoughts that feel good. Allow source to work for you and put in its path all the good desires, wants, wishes, and dreams you have. Include with them all the good feelings and emotions you have about them, and begin strengthening and building upon them to fill your pool.

Become the personal trainer of your thoughts. To have the life you wish, your thoughts must be in complete alignment with all you ask to be and want to have and experience. You must begin to allow thoughts to be of your purpose, your goals, your wishes, and your dreams. Begin creating thoughts that give you the life experience you want. To disregard a thought that does not produce an outcome of your choosing, you must recognize that thought and replace it with another more positive thought and attach to it a good feeling. It is a good exercise for you.

Those unwanted thoughts—thoughts that make you restless, uneasy, or that feel nowhere near where you want to be—must be pulled out like a weed. Give them no care just as you would pull a weed from your garden. As you practice this new way of training your mind and start having success, please know there will be thoughts you don't like, just as every healthy garden will have weeds that need pulling from time to time. So too will your mindful garden. Never allow the weeds to take over.

Exercise: You Are What You Think

Start becoming aware of your thoughts. Carry a small notebook around or use your smartphone to tally your bad thoughts versus good thoughts. As they say, if you can't measure it, you can't manage it! Now, every day, work on increasing the number of good thoughts and decreasing the number of bad thoughts. Identification is the first step!

Extra Credit!

When you feel a negative or low-vibration thought come into your mind, acknowledge it, be aware of it, and then replace it immediately with a positive thought.

Words

✧ ✧ ✧

Words are also energy.

✧ ✧ ✧

You now know the brilliant source energy that supports and surrounds you, and you can now also understand how to allow it to work for you. As we have spoken to you in regard to your feelings and emotions toward your thoughts and actions, we have yet to discuss the importance of your words: the words you have toward others and also the words you have toward yourself. Words are also energy. They require thought followed by action. There also are emotions toward the words you speak, be it in your mind or out loud, whether you are aware of this or not. Here we say again that those emotions have energy. Words spoken with emotions will create the power to allow source to begin moving toward that word and its energy.

We ask you to pay attention to your conversations: with others and also with yourself. These conversations are your story that you give to the world and those living in it. That includes you.

The words you say and the conversations you have with others are producing energy around you. What happens when words are expressed with emotions attached that are not of a good vibration and it occurs over and over? Well, you are building more power around you and those words. And it is not a power that makes for a positive life experience.

Source will see those supercharged words and want to create more of them, you see. It cares not of the emotion that surrounds it, only of the opportunity to work its magic. Source will be bringing you more similar circumstances, more of the same people, and more of the same behaviors, and will begin to present itself in new situations that materialize in your life. Do you not think that by expressing your feelings toward any circumstance, you will reap more of the same, especially if this becomes your regular story?

If this type of speaking has a pattern to it and has the feelings that show your emotions behind your words, then you are allowing it to become your prime topic, your story to share. *We say, tell a new story.* This brilliant source energy wants to produce for you what you put energy toward, so allow it to produce the story with better outcomes for yourself.

So we say to *pause.* Stop and pay very close attention to what words you put out to the world to hear. Have you paid attention to how the words and conversations made those around you feel? When you first sat with them, how was their mood? After you finished your time together, how was their mood? Was there an energy change in them? Did you also lower their vibration by holding conversations of low frequency with them? We say, yes, indeed. If they care for you and are concerned for you, then your story creates a feeling within them, so yes, it did.

This includes paying attention to *self-talk*. Many of you have conversations with yourselves. Well, actually, all of you experience self-talk to some degree. Everyone talks himself or herself into or out of something. You can convince yourself of anything with enough self-talk. It is not bad to convince yourself of anything at all as long as the energy is of a good vibration.

We wish you to understand here that what you say to yourself is also very powerful. It can empower you to perform or not. It must start with you. For others to see the greatness you are, you must first believe it within yourself first.

We are here to help you and share with you ways to better your life and create more happiness for yourself. We wish you to know that you are incredible. You are so wonderful. Life can be challenging at times. People enter your life, and things don't always work out. You will not love every job, and you will not like every boss. Not all marriages stay together. Some people have more money than others. There will always be someone who has more of something. There will be people who disappoint you and people you do not resonate with. It is true. We understand that saying these words in your story can and will produce feelings and emotions along with them that make you feel this way. We don't want you to feel down on yourself if you have been telling a story that you now see is not to your benefit. We want you to say, "It is okay." "A new day, a new way," we say. A new story creates a new life. Start writing the new story with words that, when spoken, give you an uplifting feeling. A can-do feeling. A positive feeling. Put a new twist on the current story to create a better outcome.

You are creating every plot and every outcome of your life. Being aware of your words spoken to the world and their effect in your life gives you incredible awareness of how to do it differently, with more focus and purpose toward how you want your life to be. Tell a new story for yourself with positivity and good vibes. And that is a story we very much look forward to hearing.

Exercise: Watch Your Words

Become Aware

What do your conversations sound like? What are the topics you often find yourself repeating with people? What is the story you present, through words, for people to hear and know? Is there a pattern you have regarding certain topics? When speaking about these repeated topics, do you happen to pay attention to the emotion you are expressing while speaking the words that tell the story you are sharing with others?

Have you paid much attention to the words you speak to yourself? Have you seen a pattern of talk you keep with yourself? How are you spending your conversations with *yourself*? Do you enjoy time spent hearing yourself talk about you? Are you creating conversations that are uplifting? Are these talks spent encouraging you toward a path you are excited about? If not, why not?

When you speak to yourself, what is the intention of these talks? Why are you having these conversations with yourself?

Happiness

Happiness must be felt.

Happiness is not a thing; it is not a product. It cannot be given. Happiness must be felt.

When one says you cannot look to get happiness from your mate or spouse, we say, that is not entirely so. It is true you cannot expect someone else to *give* you happiness as it is not an item to give. It can be, however, that through an action, one can give one a *reason* to be happy. It is the *intention*. Ah, we've mentioned this word before, haven't we?

We wish you to understand that it is not items that create the happiness but rather the feelings associated within yourself that bring forward the happy feelings. Having *stuff* will never create any permanent happiness. Those moments are short-lived and give little substance to draw from with any real longevity. The feelings within you from expressing yourself—through the experiences that carry with them the emotions that allow you to desire more of the good feelings—are what make for *real* happiness.

We understand some of you may disagree. You may say, "Money will make me pretty happy. Not having bills to worry about will make me pretty happy. Owning a home will make me very happy. A new car will make me so happy."

Happiness is a high-vibration frequency. It feels good. The car is energy, for example. But it has no feeling to it, so how can it be a high vibration? It cannot. It is you being in the car, experiencing the drive, having your hands on the steering wheel or feeling your hair blow in the wind of the convertible, that gives the higher vibration. It is how you choose to experience the car that gives you the happiness.

Choose to experience life from a place of high vibration. Recognize that being happy is really just a choice you make. It really is that easy to start. It is a decision, one that can and will change how you step out each day.

So how can you begin to have a happy groove? How can you start pulling forward the energy that is of a good frequency to produce the feeling of happiness for yourself? *Simply decide to go out into the world with an intention and a decision to find things that make you feel good.*

So, how does one find exactly what will *create* happiness. How does one decide? So glad you asked!

Exercise: Be Happy, Be Joyful, Be You

1. Create a List. Begin with a journal or a pad of paper, go somewhere quiet, and begin really thinking of these questions.

   a. What makes you happy?
   b. What do you love?
   c. What gives you joy?
   d. Who do you like to spend time with?
   e. What music do you enjoy?
   f. What food do you crave?
   g. What do your vacations look like?
   h. What activities do you enjoy?

   Start with simple stuff. It may be ice cream. I enjoy ice cream. It may be time with the grandchildren. When you think about your grandchildren and you feel the experiences of being with your grandchildren (which is what we wish you to do for this exercise), ask yourself if you spend enough time with them. Are you feeding yourself the high-vibration nutrition you need each day to have a happy life? This nutrition is the very stuff that does give you happiness, like being with your grandchildren, eating the ice cream, or anything else that gives you upliftment (a raise of vibration). We ask you to dig deep within yourself. Go back to the days that you can remember being more joyful. Go into the memories of the activities you once experienced that brought you to a happy day.

2. How Much of this Is Currently in Your Life? How much of this is in your daily life? Your weekly life? Your life at all? Think about the people in your life and who makes you feel good and good about yourself. How much time have you spent with them lately? When was the last time you did that activity that gave you a happy day? If you love art galleries, when did you last visit one? Do you see what we're trying to say to you here? We want you to feel your life and how you are spending your days. Are they balanced? Are you including activities for yourself each week that you look forward to?

3. Activities of Joy
We understand one must work. There are responsibilities. We understand sometimes it seems the day is over before it began and not all was finished. What we wish you

to do is take away a few things each day of the less important tasks and replace it with the joy stuff. It can be activities that require just thirty minutes. But thirty minutes here and there each day is that vibration nutrition you very much need.

4. Manage-Create-Decide-Begin
   We want you to know that you are the manager and also the creator of your day, your week, your month, your year, and your life.
   How have you been managing yourself? Have you considered yourself, your joy, and your need for happiness as you manage the days? We ask you now to take the time to make your list. We ask you now to make a one-second decision and decide to be happy. We ask you to begin managing your days and consider your joy as you make your daily schedule. We ask you to get a groove on your life and begin participating in activities that make you happy. Look at the list you made. Begin allowing your soul to dance through life and flow with the energy of happiness and feel how it truly feels to be experiencing life through it.

CHAPTER 10

Be a Seeker

Spend each day a seeker of fun. A seeker of adventure. A seeker of things to enjoy.

You may now have ideas about the things you would like to experience in your day and in your life. Some of you have begun to think and search for what *does* make you happy, what activities you may enjoy participating in, what types of things you would enjoy creating. How would you prefer to spend your free time? What areas in your life would you like to enhance? These are very good questions. We say these are the very questions that put you on a path of becoming a seeker for yourself. A seeker to everything you want, of all the emotions you want to experience. A seeker of all you hope to accomplish and how you wish to spend your days with much more joy and authenticity.

For many of you, there will be obvious thoughts that will float in that make you feel, "Yes, I would enjoy that." You will ponder some and come up with something you would like more of, whether that be freedom, money, joy, or creative outlets for yourself. It is very good to be a seeker for yourself.

Others struggle a bit here as they do know they want and need to experience more of life but are not really sure what or how. They are not sure what direction to move in to actually find it. We understand. It is difficult to know it or see it if you have not been looking for it.

Not knowing what direction to move in can be that very roadblock that has prevented this area of happiness to be more present in your life. Many have become very clear with themselves about what they do *not* like, what they do *not* want, what they no longer wish to experience. And it stops there. The roadblock keeps you in complete idle mode, and you sit in the place of all that is not working for you and spend your days stuck. Allow us to help you find a new road, a detour that can help you off the road of all you *don't* want and land you on a road of what you *do* want.

Begin going out each day with the *intention* to see things that bring you joy. This will show up in many ways. It can be that life presents you a beautiful sunrise. Do you look into the colors of the sunrise? Do you see the beauty in the tones of the different colors? Can you feel the joy within yourself if you can allow the moment to touch you? See that each day is starting with this perfect *intention* of life.

It can be found in small, simple moments, such as interactions you have with people. It could be someone's hairstyle that inspires you to try a new look for yourself, and this excites you. It can be that there were no lines at the store today, and you were served instantly. It could be that the office bought lunch today for everyone. It could be that the heat wave ended, and the cooler weather showed up, and you now appreciate the light breeze.

These things can create much more joy, much more happiness, if you let them.

Start with the small things. Start focusing and being aware of the little things that give you joy. The stuff you don't really put deep thought into but, if you did, you would feel great happiness from the simple examples we share here. Do this. Become aware of the small gifts that life gives you each day. Those gifts are packed with more gifts. One gift unfolds into another. There are always gifts within the gifts. We wish for you to open each gift that is given to you moving forward and see how it grows into more.

Spend each day as a seeker of fun. A seeker of adventure. A seeker of things to enjoy. Become aware of your experiences that are playing like a movie for you in your day each and every day. These experiences that are presented are for you to feel and see if they resonate with your soul and your heart. It is like a movie trailer playing so you can see if you would enjoy more, to see more, and experience more of it. Can you resonate with this movie? Does it move you in some positive way? Does it feel like something you would like more of?

Pay attention to the airplane that you see flying above you. Think. Where is it heading? Who is on that plane? What experiences will life present them? Then ask yourself, "Where would I want to go? Would I want a trip with relaxation or adventure? Would I stay in the country or go out of the country? How long would I go for? One week? Two weeks? Would I go alone? Is this a soul trip I would take?" Ask the questions. There is great power in asking. For when you ask, you shall discover the answers. These questions may lead you to the conclusion that you don't have a desire to travel by plane at all but you could see going by train cross-country. This asking now begins getting the motors within you purring. Do you see what we are showing you here?

You are sitting at the park. There are many people doing many things. Stop and pay attention to the movie that is playing for you in the park. Where is your focus drawn toward? Is it the man playing with his dog? As you sit and watch the joy this man and the dog are experiencing together, do you feel that it may be something you wish to have? How does it feel within you as you watch them play? Would you consider a dog to own so you can share a similar experience? Would being outdoors and playing with a dog and having that connection feel good to you? Are you missing not having an animal to love and care for? Would that bring you joy? Would you consider working as a volunteer to walk dogs that are in shelters if you cannot have one in your home? Ask yourself.

How about these three ladies who are walking laps around the park on their lunch hour from work. How does that make you feel? Does it inspire you to get a walking group together with coworkers? Do you like the idea of doing that during lunch? Is this a way you would enjoy spending your time away from the office at lunch hour? Would it give you an opportunity to bond better with a few coworkers and perhaps build a friendship? Would you like to have a stronger connection with some people at work? Ask yourself.

Do you see a person sitting under a tree, reading alone? Are you drawn toward that movie? What thoughts come to mind when you see this person reading and being content with him or herself? Do you see this person reading and wished you read more? Could you see doing this? Would you enjoy some quality alone time where you can just hang out with yourself? Ask yourself.

Life gives you movies all day long, everyday, of things that are going on around you, and we say you need to begin focusing and pay attention to the movie screen that is playing for you. Watch it. It is playing for you to inspire you, to uplift you, to build desire within you. Begin to be not just the seeker but also the question-asker.

Exercise: Watch the Movies All Around You and Rate Them

Feel each movie that plays in front of your awareness, and rate the movies with stars. The ones with a score of at least three stars or greater deserve some attention from you as there is much you can discover and learn about yourself by watching these movies and feeling the experiences of their characters. You will find many new things you enjoy and many new activities to consider when you go about life as a seeker of fun and joy.

Those with three stars and above are the very things that you should begin trying out, building upon, and including in your days to start creating a life well lived for yourself.

Discipline

Allow it to be your coach.

Do you now see how you have been managing your time each day, filling it up with things that give you limited joy? Do you feel the presence within you that says, "It is time to do things differently. It is time to try things differently. It is time to go about things differently. It is time to live a bit differently." We say, it is wonderful.

Now to be able to incorporate the processes we have laid out for you, to create that better feeling life for yourself, it is important that you provide yourself all the structure needed to build this life. We said from the beginning that we wish this book to be easy. We want it light. We wish not to make this personal journey you are on overwhelming. We want this journey to be fun. We want you to discover things about you that you love. We want you to discover activities you enjoy doing. We want you to be happy and to live your most authentic, happy self. We want you to step out each day and be excited for who you are and what you bring to the day, to the week, to the year, to yourself, and to the world. We want you to have and live the life you want, and we want you to begin creating it.

You cannot just *think* about what you would like to start experiencing in your life. Yes, you must think it, but then you must also *do it*. There must be action that moves with the thoughts if you are to create anything from them. Excuses of waiting for a better day or better weather or a more quiet home or new work schedule or the days to have more hours in them may never come. There will always be something that you can say that keeps you from your action. This is destructive self-talk at its finest. You can talk yourself out of anything. Do you think perhaps you have kept yourself on the shelf long enough, waiting for things to be different? Are you simply waiting to expire? Why are you making everything else a priority and not yourself? Why can you not really find the time for yourself? It's discipline. Here is where you must manage *yourself*.

Instead of feeling that the word *discipline* is somehow a bad word, be clear that it is just a word until you put a meaning to it that gives you an emotion about it. So, pick a new definition, a new meaning. Put a meaning to it that gives you a supercharged feeling when you think or speak of the word discipline. Allow discipline to be a motivator for you. Let the word empower you. Allow it to be your coach. A coach makes you push through the drills that help you to be successful in the game. A coach teaches the player to train correctly to have results on the field. A coach conditions you to do what need to be done to experience the win. Discipline is the way to go after your goals. It is the real force behind the action. Everything you want. All you hope to experience. All the happiness you wish to have every day is produced within the action of this word, *discipline*. It is that word that, when done, creates the structure you need to build that very foundation of the life best lived for you.

Exercise: Daily Drills

Imagine seeing the word *discipline* as an *optimistic* word. It's a word that will get you to the finish line when you put action to it. That is all. Be your own manager. Put the coach in place.

Make your daily schedule. Write each of your new daily drills of high vibrational activities, such as sitting in gratitude each day, out on paper and include the time you will do each one. Refer to it each morning and throughout the day so you are always aware of them. Put your plan to action and stick with your plan. Do not falter. Do not waiver. Do not get sidetracked. Stay focused. Stay on course and watch what happens.

Finding Your Purpose

A life's purpose is not the action; it is the emotion you feel when doing the action.

As you move through your days and weeks, at times you think, *Is this it? Is this all there is? Why am I not feeling fulfilled? Have I no purpose? Why can I not find my purpose?* You can, at times, get down on yourself and feel you have failed somehow because you have yet to discover that purpose in your life.

So many of you put a lot of pressure on yourselves about this process of locating *purpose*. It is something that must show up for you wearing this sign that says, "Here I am, your purpose, right here!" Many of you look at it like it should be something on the shelf at a store. You go in and want to get it but the shelf is empty. And it is just now out of stock, and so you wait as though a delivery will arrive and the shelf will be restocked. Purpose is not an item. It is not something that shows up on the shelf at a store, and it is not waiting for you.

We wish you to have an easy understanding of this word that gives so many of you anxiety because you think you don't have it. Many of you have been waiting for it as you would a new TV series or an anticipated e-mail. We say, purpose does not work this way.

A life's purpose is not the action; it is the emotion you *feel* when doing the action. It is not the activity; it is the feeling *behind* the activity that moves you to want more. Purpose is found within yourself, and the word is extremely wide in definition. No two people will share the same purpose even if the actions are the same. It cannot be. Each of you will experience a different degree of emotion while doing the same action that will move your soul, even if just slightly different from one another.

The activity is what gives you the action, but it is how the results of the activity make you feel. This is where the purpose you are seeking is found. It is never in the title. It is never the work but rather what is produced from the work that tells you what and where your purpose is.

Let's say you work with rescue animals. Let's say you work as a volunteer to find homes for animals with no homes. There may be several of you all working for the same cause: to find forever homes for these animals. To allow them to become pets for others is the goal and, many would say, purpose. For the organization, the purpose is finding homes for the animals.

As you work within this organization, and you bring the animal to the new owner, and you see the joy of the new pet owner, you notice the new owner to be elderly. You realize that this pet is actually companionship to this elderly person who lives alone. You realize that person now has something to give love to and something to care for every day. Neither of them are alone now. The new pet owner feels this incredible movement within of love and emotion for this action of taking in the animal, and has now been moved. This person has found purpose: something to take care of, to feed, to love, to bathe, and perhaps even to walk. It makes the person happy to have a responsibility to care for another. You deliver the new pet to the senior's home and see this interaction and realize that it was not just finding a home for the animal but it was equally giving the elderly person a way to be of service and to give love and have a reason to get out of bed. There is something now that needs this person. It gives this person such joy. You see this movie being played in front of you, and it moves you from within. You see the loving impact it has on both person and pet, and this inspires you to find more elderly people to have pets to love as you see how healing it is. This has become your purpose. It was not the action of delivering the animal but how the action unfolded that moved you emotionally. By watching this happy movie play out, it made you desire to want to do more of the same. You saw how it made someone happy and how you enjoyed the process, and this became your purpose: to help match elderly people with rescue animals.

People feel that purpose is this *big* thing. It needs to be obvious and singular: "What is this one purpose of my life?"

But here's the thing: there are *hundreds* of purposes you have in a life. It is not any one purpose that shows up. As you grow and expand, so will your purpose. We hope for you to have many purposes in many areas of your life throughout your life. We wish you to have purpose in your work, in your relationships, in your hobbies, in your volunteering, and in your parenting. Purpose can be found in all of it if you just allow yourself to feel the shifts within you and the emotions that move you to want more. Allow your good feelings to guide you in all areas of your life, and they will take you to your purpose each and every time.

Exercise: Feeling Purpose in a Moment

Think back to experiences you have had and activities you have done that created a feeling within you that felt like purpose. Make a list of these experiences you have had and reflect and feel them. Think of the moments you had with those experiences and how they affected you in a positive way.

1. How did they move you emotionally or passionately?
2. How did you feel while you were involved and engaged in the activity?
3. Were there moments you can now look back on and easily see that you felt purpose in those times?

If you enjoy being a team mom for your child's soccer team and you joyfully cut orange slices for Saturday morning's game for all the kids on the team, you can have a feeling of great purpose because you have made yourself available to many and provided needed nutrition for the children. The feeling you receive from the children's appreciation for the snack after a hard game can move you to want to do it more, and here, purpose is felt.

Now that you understand better what purpose feels like, looks like, and how it can be found (felt), can you see that you, in fact, have experienced it?

CHAPTER 13

The Soul

*It is you in your best,
brightest light.*

The soul is a big conversation as there is much that can be discussed regarding it. It could easily be a book of its own. We wish to only touch upon it for you and give you a clearer understanding about it because it is referenced many times throughout the chapters. The topic is always one that we enjoy very much as you will now feel.

The soul is you. It is you in your most beautiful, truest form. It is all that you have been and all that you are and all that lies ahead. This precious soul holds everything that you are and all that you can be. It is the place where your deepest self resides. It is always expanding and growing. It is always with you at every moment and at every breath.

It is with you during all your incarnations and also between incarnations. It is the purest part of who you are. To know yourself in the truest form, you must only look deep within to where your soul is.

There is no one exact place it sits as it is every part of your being. It can be found when you breathe, when you dream, when you rest. It is you.

To know yourself, to know your soul, you must only ask and listen. Listening is the best quality you can have to acquaint yourself with the soul.

It wants to express itself, and it does. It expresses itself each time you do something joyful, something creative, something that you gain experience from. It is there expressing itself to you, for you, and through you. It is your little voice that calls to you to listen. So listen.

Listening is important for communication with your soul for it is not a loud voice but a quiet, subtle one that requires love and attention. Being good to yourself is being good to your soul.

Food for the soul is a phrase spoken often, and its meaning is solid. You feed this soul through life, and you express yourself through it. It is the dance in your heart and the love in your heart too.

Harm is never possible on the soul; only lack of joy and lack of your truest desires may prevent it from expanding a bit. You want always to expand your soul, whether you understand that or not. It is why desires reside within you and why you have bursts of inspiration toward something. It is your voice within expressing to you the desire to expand.

The soul is a marvelous piece of you, and to know it will stop you from doubting anything again regarding your possibilities or what you are capable of achieving. For once you know this soul of yours, the deeper you, you will have an energy force that just gets empowered to go through life with a zest for surprise and curiosity and love and wellness. Once you are connected and understand who you are, you will no longer fear failures but only see excitement in attempts to try things. And the experience of new, exciting things will again expand you onto another level.

The soul can be so much conversation, but for now, know that it is the purest, best part of who you are and ever were. When we say "were," we don't mean you no longer are these things you were, as all that you have lived and expressed has served your soul well to make it the being that it is. *You.* It is the real you, the all you, the everything you. It is you in your best brightest light. It is you with all your possibilities. It is beautiful.

Exercise: Feel Your Soul Connect with You

Begin asking questions to become acquainted with your soul again. We say "again" because you have known this piece of you so many times. It is just that, in the moment, at this time, it seems dug deep inside and difficult to find. To start digging it out, you must only ask to know it and then become aware of things that bring happiness to you.

Begin searching and discovering things that make you laugh and also cry. Crying is a beautiful way to connect with your soul as it is meant to express emotions. Emotions are our barometer of how we feel and are directly connected to our souls. So feel. Feel your way into yourself. Feel excitement (find what excites you), feel the pain if something feels sad to you. Feel the beauty of something you see that is visually stimulating to you. Feel the words of a song that moves you. These are wonderful exercises to connect with your best, highest self. The all that you really are.

Love Yourself

*Show love to yourself, for
it is the greatest nourishment
you can give yourself.*

We want for you to spend your days in a vibration that feels good. To walk in and out of any day with the frequency of high vibration feels very good. *Love* is the highest-vibration word, and within it are many more feelings with words that are birthed from it. Their associated vibrations share a similar energy frequency. As the saying goes, "Birds of a feather flock together." High vibration hangs around other high vibrations. To be in and around the energy of love is life being expressed at its most brilliant for you. It radiates light for you.

If there was one word we say that most of you deeply search for it is *love*. It is the feeling you receive when in the vibration of love that creates the yearning. You must go within yourself to truly have it and truly feel it to deeply know it. There is much to love in many things within you, and if you can understand this and begin seeing this yourself with love, and start responding to it by giving love from within you to yourself, then that vibration will begin to flow in and through your day.

Love is not just *one thing* or *one feeling*. Think of love as a beautiful ocean, overflowing with life. There are coral reefs, fish of all sizes; there are starfish and pebbles, rocks, seaweed, salt, and even mammals. So too does love have many degrees of feelings held in it, such as affection, tenderness, and devotion. The ocean is enormous, and within it lives much. Love too is enormous, and within it too lives much. The ocean would not have the same impact if all within it were not there. It is the same with love.

We say, be in love with yourself. Show love to yourself, for it is the greatest nourishment you can feed yourself. By loving yourself, you then have the know-how to love others and to recognize love in all areas. Then you can shine that love to all things and express yourself from the deeper self in the exact way you were made to: with love always.

To have love, to feel love, to understand love, to recognize love you, must know it. To know it, you must be it. To be a part of love is the best way to connect with it. So we ask: Do you love you? Do you feel affectionate toward yourself and how you see yourself? Do you have deep affection for the dreams in your heart and how you wish to live them? Have you thought about yourself this way? Are you good to yourself? How do you treat yourself? Can you feel any love in the things you do well or not well? What can you find to love about you? Can you feel love in the reasons you do the things you do? What do you love most about yourself? What qualities of yours shine? Can you see your unique qualities? Do you feel love for those qualities?

Ponder this a moment. Sit a bit and think about this. Love is about expressing yourself in the truest, deepest way. It is about loving who you are. *Love* is a very big word, and a very powerful vibration holds it. Yet few go into the understanding of where love sits within the person. Love is expression. It wants to be recognized. You are love. Do you recognize it?

Exercise: The Quality of Love

- Are you tender toward yourself?
- Are you gentle with your words to yourself?
- Do you allow yourself to rest if you need rest?
- Are you affectionate with yourself? Do you tell yourself you look good?
- Do you feel good about the things you have done or accomplished in a day, in your life, or even in a moment? Do you say, "Good job!" to yourself?
- Are you loyal to yourself and your needs?
- Are you grateful for the qualities you have that you enjoy about yourself?
- Are you committed to yourself to do things that are good for your happiness and well-being?

These are all acts of love.

Write down ten things you love about yourself. Say them out loud to yourself each day. Ponder each quality you have and think about how it has improved your life as well as the lives of people around you.

CHAPTER 15

Arriving

We want you to know that you are capable of everything you wish to be, for you are all this already. It is your time to discover it.

Our hope for you after reading this book is that you can begin to walk toward life with ease. We want for you to be light. To not have heaviness within you that you must fight through. We want you to know that all is well.

We wish for you to go through your days with excitement and see the gifts that present themselves all around you. To open your eyes to the beauty that you truly are. You are magnificent. You are perfect. You are a part of everything, and everything is a part of you. We want you to understand that you have an incredible support system working for you every single minute of every single day. It is there for you, guiding you and supporting you and giving you direction toward things that feel better, things that feel good, things that are for you to experience with joy. Pay attention. Be aware of it.

We want you to know that you are capable of everything you wish to be, for you are all this *already*. It is your time to discover it. To understand that life throws you circumstances to grow from and experiences to feel from. To see the circumstances as part of life giving you ways to find yourself, your happiness. There has been much good for you even when you could not see it.

Remember that each day is an Oscar-winning movie that plays for you, to speak to you and show you things for you to take notice of. You can discover more of the things you want and more of things that move you within, that inspire you to go in a direction toward that which is meant for you. Trust it. Allow yourself to be the character in that movie that you watch and to feel the experience to decide if that experience is for you. "Does this feel good to me? Shall I try this? Shall I do that?" Life is always giving you ideas to pursue and try. Life wants you to be a seeker. Life is always showing up each day to motivate you and to stir something from within you to take action.

We want you to understand that happiness is meant for everyone. Life is to be lived and enjoyed each day. A need for better balance and more fun must be in your days. You are so much more than a progression of joyless tasks, one after the other.

We know that as you begin taking the steps in our book and apply them to your life, you will find your happiness. You will live with more joy. You will love who you are, and you will ignite the passion that sits dormant in you. We are excited for your journey of self. We are excited you have now arrived at this place to begin your excursions and start playing and enjoying your life. We wish you to always be on a journey of finding joy, of feeling love, of knowing more of who you are.

For as you continue on this personal road trip to self, you will always discover more ways to happiness. And you will begin knowing more and more of the things that give you joy; and you will love who you are and enjoy being with yourself.

Stay on this road, for as you do, beautiful scenes will increasingly show up for you to ponder, be inspired by, find desire in. It will lead you to more and more places that feel amazing to you, and that will give you what you crave to feel, to experience, and to be. Life is a journey, a wonderful journey, and you are the driver. Stay focused! The road may throw up some pebbles from time to time, but you can see now that they are only placed there to grab your attention.

Always navigate yourself to what feels good. Stay on that road, and it will lead you to a life that is full of high vibration. A life much enjoyed. We are very excited for you and all that will be.

With much love,
Edgar and Monica

For Those Wanting More

If you would like to connect with Monica, you can visit her website at www. MonicaTeurlings.com. To get updates on upcoming news and events, we welcome you to go to her social media pages and become a fan of her Facebook page: Monica Teurlings Psychic Medium or follow her on Instagram at monicateurlingspsychicmedium

If you are interested in participating in a weekend workshop focused on deepening the material from the book, please go to the workshop page on her website for more information on upcoming events. If there is not a workshop offered in your area but you would like one, please contact her through e-mail.

The process laid out in this book will help those who are looking to better their lives. When they feel better, they perform better. If you have a company and would like Monica to come and teach a two-day workshop for your employees, please e-mail her directly at info@MonicaTeurlings.com